THE PHILOSOPHY AND PRACTICES OF KRIYA YOGA

ROY EUGENE DAVIS

Let us acknowledge that radiant light of the Supreme Reality. May it reveal our true path in life, illumine our minds, and unfold in our consciousness the liberating knowledge of absolute truth.

CSA PRESS, PUBLISHERS
CENTER FOR SPIRITUAL AWARENESS
Lakemont, Georgia 30552

CSA Press, Publishers
Post Office Box 7
Lakemont, Georgia 30552

CSA Press is the publishing department of
Center for Spiritual Awareness. Offices and
retreat center are on Lake Rabun Road
in Lakemont, Georgia 30552
Telephone (706) 782-4723
Fax (706) 782-4560

PRINTED IN THE UNITED STATES OF AMERICA

Contents

By knowing the causative principles
of life and cooperating with them, we
can live in lasting happiness, good health,
and perfect harmony with God and nature.
We are on this earth for but a little
while, and the real reason for our being
here is very different from what we
may have imagined.

    – *Paramahansa Yogananda*

Introduction

The Path of Light

The purpose of this small book is to provide an overview of the essential practices of this direct way to authentic spiritual growth which allows the fulfillment of all of life's primary purposes. Even a little study of what is here presented will improve the reader's understanding; dedicated personal application of the principles and practices can be transformative and illuminating.

For all of us, there is nothing to know or experience in this or any realm that is as important as being consciously aware of our true relationship with the Infinite. When this condition is partially apprehended, everyday circumstances are naturally improved. When it is fully realized, permanent soul satisfaction results.

That there is an enlivening Power nurturing the universe, with which we can have a responsive relationship, is the testimony of saints and the assurance of our present and future good. On our sojourn in space and time, the circumstances of our lives are often determined by our personal choices. Let us always choose the path of light.

Roy Eugene Davis

March 7 & 9, 1995
Lakemont, Georgia
U.S.A.

CHAPTER ONE

Every Soul's Compelling Aspiration

The primary instinct of life is a desire for continued, conscious, enjoyable existence—for fulfilled, immortal life. Our awareness of this compelling instinct reveals the fact of our divine origins; at a deep level we know our inmost nature is spiritual and we yearn to have its innate knowledge and capacities actualized by having our awareness restored to wholeness and the freedom it provides.

Some people move almost effortlessly in the direction of spiritual fulfillment. Life, for them, is a progressive series of unfolding, fortunate events which seem as though predestined or made possible by evidential grace. Others, their minds troubled by confusion and conflict, experience sequential episodes of misfortune that feed their anxieties, cause them heartache and emotional unrest, and elicit in them symptoms of apathy and despair. Regardless of present, personal circumstances, every person has the same core nature, the same potential for growth and unfoldment, and the same eventual, ultimate spiritual-fulfillment destiny.

Whether spiritual awakening and actualization is slow, moderately progressive, or rapid, depends somewhat upon one's psychological and physical condition, aptitude to learn and capacity to apply what is learned, and the will to excel or its absence. For a person who is capable of choosing to live a constructive, intentional life, spiritual awakening and actualization of soul knowledge and capacities can be rapid. Such a one will intelligently choose to implement actions which allow desired results to be experienced or demonstrated within a relatively brief duration of time. This is the direct way to psychological transformation, rapid spiritual growth, and the fulfillment of life's primary purposes. This is the way of *Kriya Yoga*, the way that effectively removes all mental, physical, and circumstantial obstacles to spiritual growth and the unfoldment and expression of soul abilities and capacities.

Kriya is a Sanskrit word for any "action" we implement or perform for the purpose of facilitating our overall wellness, effective function, and spiritual growth. The word *yoga* is derived from the Sanskrit verb *yuj*, which occurs in several forms according to its intended usage. It can mean "to join," "to restrain," or "to regulate or keep under control,"as in yoking or connecting. It can also mean "to bring together" one's attention with an object perceived or contemplated. Another meaning is the end result of endeavor or practice: "completion," "oneness," or "wholeness." When engaged in self-improvement regimens for any purpose, we are engaged in the *practice* of yoga. When the purpose has been accomplished, we are *established* in the yoga of the end result.

While familiarity with the word-meanings of *kriya* and *yoga* is helpful, it is not necessary for everyone on the spiritual growth path to cultivate extraordinary language skills in order to live effectively and fulfill life's primary purposes. Of greater value is to learn and apply the principles and procedures which can enable one to undergo desired or needed transformational changes, be successful in chosen, constructive endeavors of every kind, and experience satisfying spiritual growth as a result of orderly unfoldments of soul qualities. Living like this is the very essence of the way of Kriya Yoga, just as it is the essence of every valid "way" that has been spontaneously revealed or is accurately represented as being supportive of improved personal circumstances and the nurturing of authentic spiritual growth.

Because we are innately inclined to want to experience continued, conscious, enjoyable existence, it is natural for us to desire to be spiritually aware, mentally alert and competent, emotionally mature, physically healthy, in supportive relationship to others and our environment, functional and effective in endeavors, and successful in having our primary purposes fulfilled. Our approach to living should be intelligently chosen, regulated by reason and common sense, and balanced in performance of actions as determined by our aspiration to experience wholeness. In this way we will live with enlightened (knowledgeable) understanding and every moment, though but an incident in the field of Great Time or eternity, will be appreciated and enjoyed. Therefore, it will be useful now to review the primary purposes of life which are to be fulfilled while we are yet in relationship to the natural order. When they are fulfilled, we are enabled to live in this or any world as the free beings we essentially are. When they are denied or are unfulfilled, degrees of limitation and unhappiness result.

1. *To Have Harmonious, Cooperative Relationships with Others and with Causative Principles and Supportive Influences of Nature* – When all relationships are ideal and we are living with conscious, purposeful intention, righteousness (rightness, orderliness) prevails. The characteristics of this condition are peace of mind, soul contentment, friendly accord with people and environmental conditions, easy accomplishment of endeavors, and the full support of the totality and actions of nature. We then know that we are "in our right place in the universe," doing and experiencing exactly what is best for us to do and experience at every moment and in every situation. We should choose an entirely constructive lifestyle which includes supportive relationships of all kinds, work or service that is life-enhancing for all who are influenced by it, wholesome habits and behaviors, a natural food diet plan, and a balance of activity and rest.

2. *To Have Desires Easily Fulfilled* – The desires to restrain or renounce (release or let go) are those which are not in accord with our higher purposes, which will waste our time and resources, or will cause us or others unhapppiness or misfortune. Legitimate desires can easily be fulfilled by skillful exercise of creative imagination, sustained faith, and knowledgeable endeavor. As we become more aware of our relationship with the universe,

including Universal Mind in which the cosmos exists, we can discover that the mere impulse of desire or the existence of a need draws a response from the universe that serves to fulfill our desires and satisfy our needs. The reason for this universal action is that, when we are spiritually aware and any circumstance somewhat disturbs our soul peace, the forces of nature favorably respond so that we can be restored to a peaceful state.

All restrictions and obstacles to fulfillment should be eliminated by reason, intuition, creative imagination, concentrated endeavor, and absolute trust in God and in the responsiveness of nature.

3. *To Be Affluent* – To be "in the flow of the natural rhythms, evolutionary trends, and fortuitous events of life" is to spontaneously demonstrate affluence. Attention given to the basic matters already mentioned are helpful to this end. The truth about us is that, whether we are aware of it or not, we already exist in the omnipresent field of the One Consciousness we call God. Therefore, if there is any lack in our lives it must be due to our inability (or unwillingness) to perceive and experience what is already available for us to apprehend and actualize.

As is an undiscerning or impractical person who remains thirsty, hungry, or impoverished in the midst of an abundance of fresh water, food, and available resources, so are we when we affirm lack or limitation while presently existing in the wholeness of life. By acquiring accurate information about ourselves and our true relationship with God and the universe, and by right application of knowledge and appropriate living, we can learn to experience affluence. We can learn to thrive, flourish, and be successful in every way—if we really want to.

4. *To be Self-Realized and God-Conscious* – Comfortable, affluent self-conscious or egocentric existence is not the highest purpose for which we are in this world. Millions of people are healthy, reasonably comfortable, and sufficiently affluent to live without having to struggle to survive, and are not yet completely fulfilled because they are not as spiritually awake as they can be. We are spiritual beings only temporarily relating to the mundane realm. We have a Spirit-mind-body relationship to God and the universe. Our spiritual nature is superior to our mental and physical characteristics.

The immortal Self of us is a ray of God's consciousness individualized. We are not independent units of consciousness separate from or apart from God; we are specialized aspects of the One Being from which souls and all of nature emanate. To be fully aware of ourselves in relationship to God and the universe is to be Self-realized. To be fully aware that God is our omnipresent, omnipotent, omniscient reality is to be God-conscious. Until we are Self-realized and God-conscious, our endeavors to live effectively provide us a stable foundation upon which to base our lives and from which to expand awareness to apprehension and comprehension of higher realities. When we are Self-realized and God-conscious, we are enabled and empowered to live spontaneously and appropriately without self-conscious endeavor to do so.

We are living in a world in which millions of people are rapidly awakening to levels of awareness from which higher possibilities can be glimpsed. Societal changes are occurring in ways heretofore unknown in the history of humankind on the planet. It is, therefore, necessary for thoughtful, caring individuals to educate themselves about matters related to their personal welfare and functional effectiveness, and about higher mental and spiritual realities, so that spiritual growth occurs more rapidly than evolutionary unfoldments in the outer realm. We should not be content to keep abreast of our changing times; we should be able to foresee events by improving our understanding of the causative forces which drive them. For this, we need to awaken quickly from self-conscious levels of awareness to superconscious, cosmic conscious, and God-conscious levels.

Seek first knowledge and realization of God, and live so that you are in harmony with the supportive actions of evolution and grace; and all things necessary for your well-being will be provided for you.

– *The Gospel According to Saint Matthew 6:33*

CHAPTER TWO

A Return to Wholeness

Spiritual awareness is not a condition we create or accomplish; it is directly realized when our attention is returned to awareness of the already-wholeness of our soul consciousness. At the soul level we are Self-complete, serene, knowledgeable, and flawless. When we know how to return attention to soul awareness and choose to do so—and during episodes of spontaneous transcendence of sensory and mental states—Self-knowledge can be immediately experienced. The fact of the present accessibility of the soul-aware state is proof of its reality and constancy. Once this is known to us, we can learn to adjust our viewpoints and states of consciousness at will, by choice and gentle intention. By becoming proficient in practice, we are enabled to acquire mastery of states of consciousness, mental and emotional states, physical states, and of personal circumstances. By choosing a life of excellence and learning how to demonstrate it, we can live in harmonious cooperation with the Power that enlivens the universe, directs the course of human events, and ensures the fulfillment of soul destiny.

The cause of diminished soul awareness is obsessive identification with self-conscious states and mental conditionings. This causes attachments to one's mistaken sense of self-identity, rigid beliefs, misperceptions, mental transformations and processes, moods, physical perceptions and sensations, and environmental conditions. The solution to the problem of self-consciousness (egocentric fixation) which contracts awareness and clouds the intellect is to engage in a program of self-training for the purpose of restoring soul awareness to wholeness. This will result in: 1) awakening to clear levels of awareness; 2) elimination of erroneous beliefs (delusions) and errors in perception (illusions); 3) the resisting, weakening, and removal of destructive, self-diminishing mental conditionings; 4) emotional maturity characterized by self-responsible behaviors; 5) cessation of confusion and restlessness which, when ordinarily influential, contributes to persistent, unregulated mental transformations and modifications; 6) the ability to live naturally and constructively as determined by higher understanding directed by innate, soul impulses to experience enjoyable, fulfilling activities and relationships.

The final fulfillment is liberation of consciousness from blind identification with all conditions which formerly clouded and fragmented soul awareness. Then permanently established in Self-knowledge, our awareness is not subject to environmental, physical, or mental-emotional influences. Discontent or suffering are no longer possible, neither in the moment nor in the future.

To the extent that we are capable of realizing it, the liberated state is to be experienced and actualized here and now, rather than to be idealized as a possible future condition. We do not have to depart from this world in order to be liberated; we have only to withdraw from involvements (including delusions, illusions, and conflicted mental-emotional states) with conditions and circumstances, and relationships if necessary, which might modify our awareness or inhibit or restrict our ability to creatively function.

A liberated person naturally lives a spontaneously appropriate life: perceptions are flawless, thinking is rational, emotions are regulated, behaviors are ethical and moral, relationships are wholesome and supportive, actions are purposeful, and a state of cosmic or universal consciousness is stable. Until Self-realized and God-conscious, the spiritual aspirant is advised to remain alert to the need to cultivate intellectual powers, maintain constructive mental states, regulate emotions and moods, choose a lifestyle which is entirely supportive of soul-inspired aims and purposes, become proficient in apprehending the presence and reality of God, and to consider everything that is done as spiritual practice. In this way there will be no sense of separation between everyday life and the spiritual life. An obstacle to spiritual growth commonly self-created by many people is that of living their lives as conditioned, habit-bound beings, instead of comprehending the usefulness of living every waking moment from soul awareness. In truth, almost anyone who affirms a desire to live a more soul-centered life, and to demonstrate the benefits of such behavior, can do it almost immediately if they will but choose to do so and remain committed to their choice.

It is helpful to understand that there is a fundamental difference between "ordinary awareness" and "consciousness." *Ordinary awareness* is awareness of something, of subjective mental-emotional processes or of objective things, relationships, events, or circumstances. *Consciousness* is the agency in and through which awareness functions. Consciousness is changeless; awareness is subject to fluctuation, modification, and transformation. Our spiritual nature, then, is pure consciousness which remains ever what it is. When we are stable in pure consciousness we are soul content and capable of being the observer of transient events. When we are not stable in experience of pure consciousness, awareness is inclined to be identified with shifting mental states, mood changes, sensory perceptions, and external relationships of various kinds. When the distinction between ourselves as pure consciousness and our awareness as identified with externals is blurred or dimmed, we may forget our real, changeless nature and become involved without discernment in situations which further confuse awareness and cause us discomfort.

The first step in the direction of liberation of consciousness, then, is to endeavor to understand the philosophical basis upon which spiritual practices are founded: 1) that there is an obvious difference between the soul as consciousness and that of which the soul is aware; 2) this difference can be known by analyzing the situation, and definitely experienced by entering into an experimental process that provides opportunities to withdraw awareness from objects of attachment and return it to wholeness.

The end result of practice is the disentanglement of awareness from all that consciousness is not, so that pure consciousness can be self-revealed for what it is—the eternal, changeless essence and reality of our being. When this is intellectually or intuitively apprehended, it is easy to understand why all endeavors to create or develop spiritual awareness must fail. We can improve our mental skills and functional abilities—and we should, to be enabled to live effectively and accomplish chosen or agreed upon purposes—but what we are, as pure conscious beings, remains apart from physical and mental circumstances, as a witness of them. When consciousness is detached from conditioned states of awareness, and from egoism (the sense of independent selfhood), it remains alone as what it is, without need of any supporting condition.

Appropriate spiritual practices—which may vary somewhat according to the devotee's personal circumstances, psychological state, temperament, and aptitude for learning and applying what is learned—result in transforming and clearing the devotee's awareness. Fragmented, conflicted states of awareness are transformed as powers of concentration improve, confusion is replaced by lucid comprehension, and intellectual and intuitive insights provide glimpses of realities outside of the field or domain of ordinary states of awareness. Erroneous beliefs, misperceptions, continuing shifting of mental states and of moods, constant sensory input and its impact upon mental and emotional states, tend to keep the average person in a constant state of unease or discontent.

When the distinction between pure conscious-ness and ordinary states of awareness is obscured, one may be depressed or apathetic. There may be an inclination to strongly identify oneself only with mental-emotional states. There may be an inclina-tion to become attached to pleasant experiences and situations. Fear of death may also prevail, with aspiration for soul unfoldment sometimes mixed with a wish for unconsciousness and cessation of existence.

The practical means for overcoming all obstacles to psychological transformation and spiritual growth can be learned and applied by any person capable of making choices who is willing to be committed to the processes. The direct approach includes: 1) disciplined, repeated practice on both a theoretical and experimental, practical level; 2) renunciation of secular and subjective attach-ments of all kinds; 3) devotion to and meditation upon selected ideals or objects of concentration; 4) the use of techniques and regimens to nurture faith, enhance physical vitality and function, im-prove memory and other mental skills, facilitate super-conscious experiences, awaken intuition, and in all ways restore awareness to wholeness by allowing experience of pure consciousness. Along with these intentional practices one is advised to study philosophical principles, live simply with con-structive intention, and endeavor to integrate into everyday relationships and behaviors what is learned and experienced.

The recommended foundation practice for a

spiritual aspirant is meditation, regularly included in the daily routine and practiced for the purpose of eliciting superconscious states and experiencing their transformative influences. Meditation is practiced by sitting quietly, internalizing attention, concentrating upon a chosen point of focus, and contemplating without distraction until a shift of awareness occurs which allows unfoldments of superconscious states. Some meditators can easily experience spontaneous inwardness and awakening. Most beginning meditators have difficulty in practicing effectively because their awareness is too involved with physical and mental processes. A variety of physical and mental techniques have been discovered which, when successfully used, cause beneficial physical changes, constructive mental transformations, and adjustments of states of consciousness so that awareness is naturally withdrawn from distracting circumstances and becomes clear. The experience of clear states of self-conscious awareness, while restful and useful, are preliminary to superconscious states which are unfolded when meditation practice is continued with alert attention. Superconscious states are degrees of soul awareness that are experienced when the distinction between ordinary, fragmented awareness and pure consciousness is apprehended or transcended.

In keeping with the ideal of integrating learned or discovered knowledge into every life and circumstances, several practical modes for actualizing this are recommended. These may be referred to as yogas, disciplines, procedures, practices, or ways:

1. *The Way of Attentiveness* – Knowing that when we are not Self-aware we are inclined to experience clouded or blurred awareness and its effects (unintentional involvement with irrational mental processes, mood swings, misperceptions, and misguided behaviors), a helpful practice is to be attentive as the witness and experiencer in relationship to our thoughts, feelings, observations, behaviors, and circumstances. In this way we can remain soul-centered in the midst of day-to-day activities, appropriately relate to whatever occurs, avoid conflict and stress, and function purposefully and effectively.

2. *The Way of Nonattachment* – By remaining attentive and insightful, we can perform all actions, enjoy relationships and outcomes of endeavors, and accomplish chosen purposes successfully without egocentric identification with actions, or attachment to them or their results. This is sometimes referred to as "being in the world but not of it" and as "wearing worldliness as one wears a loose garment." We can be curious, interested, and productive, always with a light touch because of clear understanding. To this end it is helpful to remember that nothing of the realm of nature is permanent; that we are but sojourners in space and time; that the physical realm is not our origin.

3. *The Way of Knowledge* – Whether meditating or when engaged in everyday activities and relationships, we can learn by practice to see through all delusions, illusions, and outer appear-

ances, to the core of reality. In this way we can know that one Being, Life, Power, and Substance is supporting the drama of nature as well as expressing as it, and that we are, at our inmost level of being, a flawless, particularized unit of pure consciousness. This is the absolute truth—not to merely be believed, but to be directly known and experienced.

4. *The Way of Devotion* – Where our treasure is, there is our attention and commitment. Our priorities are always known to us as determined by our thoughts, aspirations, desires, involvements, and actions. We always do what we feel is most important to our well-being or what we think will satisfy our real or imagined needs. By being devoted to the ideal of wholesome, constructive living, continued learning, and spiritual growth, we are enabled to remain steadfast on the soul awakening path. The highest ideal is to awaken to knowledge and experience (realization) of the entire range of consciousness, from the transcendental level of absolute existence to its varied universal manifestations. To awaken to this experience is to be fully enlightened. Until full enlightenment, we can be devoted to God, to progressive spiritual growth, and to selfless, compassionate service to others and the rhythms and flows of evolution. In this way we become cooperative participants in the ongoing processes of life. As we live in harmony with evolutionary forces, they nurture and provide for us, and contribute to our more rapid spiritual growth. It is by living as we know best that we put ourselves into relationship with the Infinite and its resources.

All that we need for our welfare and fulfillment is already available to us; we have only to learn to be in harmonious accord with it.

Wholeness is the permanent condition of life. When our awareness is no longer conflicted and fragmented, direct experience of this fact is our clear realization. Train yourself to think and act as an alert, functional person in harmony with life as a wholeness. Artificial boundaries which formerly separated you from friendly relationships and supportive good fortune will vanish. You will know your mind to be but a fragment of Universal Mind with which you have cooperative interactions and that you are forever established in God.

Consider it natural to grow spiritually and to have awareness cleared so that Self-knowledge unfolds and functional abilities are easily and skillfully utilized. You are in this world to live as a free being. Learn how to do it. You can, because the knowledge and power of God in you is ever inclined to manifest and express its potential.

When soul liberation is realized, the devotee is removed from all troublesome circumstances, all aspirations of the heart are fulfilled, and the ultimate purpose of life is accomplished.

– *Sri Yukteswar (guru of Paramahansa Yogananda)*

CHAPTER THREE

Timeless Guidelines to Effective Living and Rapid Spiritual Growth

Because the problem of clouded awareness common to the human condition is universal, the way to spiritual awakening and growth remains the same through the ages. There are no new ways to realize the enlightened state; there are only direct and indirect ways. In this book I am explaining the direct way which has been taught by sages and seers for thousands of years.

1. *Renounce Violence, Live Harmlessly* – The ideal is not only to refrain from harmful acts of any kind, but also to be devoid of thoughts, feelings, tendencies and inclinations to injure oneself, others, creatures, or nature. When acts which might cause pain, discomfort, or inconvenience are necessary, they can be performed efficiently and dispassionately. The main thing is for us to avoid doing anything which in any way diminishes life's inclination to fulfill its purposes, while doing those things which enhance our lives, the lives of others, and of all aspects of nature. When we are consistent in harmlessness, we are on friendly, cooperative terms with a friendly world. We are nurtured and supported by others and the very processes of life, as we are nurturing and supportive of them.

2. *Be Established in Truthfulness* – To confront the facts of life, and of ourselves, is to be truthful. To endeavor to suppress or evade the facts is to be untruthful. Two obvious examples of untruthfulness are habitual lying and deceitful behaviors, both of which are characteristic of emotional immaturity. As untruthfulness produces and maintains mental and emotional conflict, its opposite contributes to peace of mind, emotional balance, and an open rapport with life on all levels. Where there is untruth, there is darkness and despair because knowledge is hidden and creative life processes are restricted. Where there is truth, there is the light of understanding, and happiness because no barriers to apprehension of knowledge exist and creative forces and actions can flow without interference.

To be able and willing to confront the facts of life (the truth) is essential to successful living and spiritual growth. Denial of the reality of God is the most self-damaging evasion of the truth because it results in denial of ourselves and others as spiritual beings and in misperceptions of the underlying characteristics and purposes of the universe. When we are established in truthfulness, nothing is hidden from us. Because wholeness is perceived and experienced, nothing is lacking; restrictions and limitations cease to be experienced.

3. *Be Self-Reliant* – The foundation principle of self-reliance is to be soul and God-reliant. Because we are immortal spirits forever to express God's characteristics, we do not have to want for anything. With this realization we will not think in terms of

competition or unfulfilled needs, or be inclined to desire to take from another what is theirs by right of their own fate or endeavor. Knowledgeable and competent, decisive and courageous, we will experience our own relationship with life, creating or attracting what is ours by right of our states of unclouded awareness, constructive mental states, and skillful actions. When we are established in self-knowledge, our reliance is upon That of which we are but expressions which made provision for us when the worlds were patterned in Universal Mind before their material manifestation.

4. *Wisely Use Vital Forces and Resources for Higher Purposes* – The vital forces of the soul enliven mind and body and make possible our creative actions and expressions. When conserved and directed to purposeful ends they make possible the accomplishment of endeavors, contribute to overall health and vitality, empower mental faculties, enliven the nervous system, and support our aspirations to further soul awakening and actualization of innate abilities. Balanced lifestyle routines of scheduled activity and deep rest; nutritious diet; wholesome habits; mental peace and emotional calm; ethical behaviors; purposefulness and accomplishment; and meditative contemplation of higher realities, are actions and behaviors which are supportive of us. Erratic lifestyle routines; insufficient rest; accumulation of stress; ingestion of nutrient-deficient foods; unwholesome habits which deplete vital forces (including self-indulgence in worry and other obsessive behaviors); dishonest or confused

behaviors; purposelessness; and choosing to conform to attitudes, relationships, and behaviors common to self-conscious or egocentric awareness, are self-defeating actions to be avoided. A commonsense guide to personal behavior is: if what is thought, felt, or done is life-enhancing and clears and expands awareness, allow it; if what is thought, felt, or done is life-suppressing and clouds awareness, avoid it.

5. *Be Expansive and Compassionate* – When our awareness opens to cosmic perceptions, we can more clearly see ourselves in ideal relationships to our world and others. Small-minded, self-centered, grasping or possessive attitudes and behaviors are unworthy of us as spiritual beings; they are nurtured by egoism, insecurity, self-righteousness, and inclinations to demonstrate personal power and control over others and circumstances. Life is whole; there is a right place in the universe for us, and for everyone and everything that contributes to the overall good. By discovering where and how we are best suited to function in the universe, we are enabled to fulfill our mundane purposes and our spiritual destiny without conflict or discord. As we are appreciative of our opportunities to learn, grow, and serve the cause of evolution, so we should bless others with our thoughts and actions that they might be enabled to be open to their opportunities to learn, grow, and participate. While fulfilling our known purposes, we can assist others to know and fulfill theirs. Compassionate behaviors are spontaneous when we clearly acknowledge that the true

nature of others is identical to our own; that we share a common foundation-source in God and a common destined awakening in God.

6. *In All Circumstances, Let Purity Prevail* – The practical value of a pollution-free environment, personal hygiene, wholesome habits, and regulated lifestyle routines is obvious. Of equal value is mental purity because of insightful self-understanding, intentional cultivation of optimism, constructive rational thinking, spiritual practices which allow superconscious influences to beneficially act upon and transform mental states, and the spontaneous actions of enlivening soul forces impelled by inner grace because of the soul's urge to have awareness returned to wholeness. The end result of purity of mind is the removal of inertia and cloudiness which obscures the soul's perception of its true nature and tends to confine awareness to the unregulated actions of the mind caused by restlessness and confusion.

7. *Learn to Always Be Soul-Content* – We are established in soul contentment when calmly anchored in awareness of ourselves as spiritual beings in the field of God's consciousness. We are then inwardly happy regardless of outer conditions or circumstances—which we intuitively know to be but temporary. Our capacity to be soul-content is not dependent upon externals; it is experienced by personal choice and gentle intention. After deep meditation, the after-effects of meditative calm can be maintained for a duration. At other times, when-

ever we become aware that we are too outwardly involved, challenged, stressed, or distracted, we can return awareness to our center of being and be peaceful. Soul contentment is not the same as being apathetic, bored, disinterested, or choosing to avoid circumstances by clinging to illusions; it is the natural result of right under-standing and Self-identity. Established in soul contentment we can solve all problems which challenge, while maintaining mental clarity and emotional poise.

8. *Be Analytical and Self-Disciplined, to Experience Psychological Transformation and Unfold and Actualize Spiritual Capacities* – The enlightenment path is not for people who are careless or lazy, or who prefer delusions and illusions to truth. Honest self-analysis is necessary if soul consciousness is to be discerned as being other than ordinary, conflicted states of awareness. We need to know the contents of the mind; the drives and tendencies which contribute to purposeless behaviors; the hurts and traumas to be healed; and what is essential to our wellness, spiritual growth, and success in life. We need to know why and how to live our lives effectively. Self (soul)-directed behaviors are to be cultivated in order to weaken and eliminate suppressive or restrictive psychological characteristics. When these obstacles to Self-knowledge and creative expression are removed, life is easily and spontaneously experienced as it is meant to be demonstrated. The direct approach to self-disciplined behaviors is to avoid all habits of thinking, feeling, relating, and doing, that are not useful to

higher ends—while cultivating and perfecting mental-emotional states, relationships, and behaviors which are entirely supportive of our aspirations for growth and illumination of consciousness.

9. *Be Diligent in Spiritual Practices* – Our lives will be in tune with the Infinite and all endeavors will be more successful when regular meditation practice is included as a priority in our schedule of daily self-care routines. Intentional, meditative spiritual practices can include prayer, the use of helpful techniques for the purpose of eliciting physical relaxation and mental calm, contemplation of transcendental realities, surrender to spontaneous unfoldments of superconscious states, and any other supportive, awareness-clearing processes. At other times, we can be steadfastly resolved to live our lives with alert, conscious intention and be relaxed and cheerful while doing this. Living should be enjoyable and purposeful. (Meditation practices will be described in more detail later in this text.)

10. *Have Faith in God* – From an egocentric perception of everyday circumstances it may seem that our lives are our own to live and that people, things, and circumstances are to be used for our personal purposes. It is a mistake to believe this.

The truth is, our lives are not our own and we possess nothing. At the level of clear soul knowing, God is apprehended as the reality of us and of everything—wholeness *is*; separation or otherness is not. We can take this information on faith— because enlightened men and women of the ages have shared it as their understanding and we intuitively know it to be so—until we have examined, tested, and proved it by our personal experience. And this is precisely what we are compelled by our innate urge in the direction of fulfillment to do.

When we have a sincere desire to experience the reality of God, it is easier for us to live a natural life directed by our intelligence. For steadfastness on the soul awakening path, three disciplines need to be observed: physical, moral, and spiritual. Wholesome lifestyle routines should be cultivated to nurture physical health and maintain the body in a functional state. Healthy, long life has value because it enables us to accomplish our secular and spiritual purposes. Appropriate, ethical behavior is essential to supportive relationships and to psychological health. Attention given to these two disciplines will enable a person to live an honorable, comfortable, and successful human life and will allow moderate spiritual growth to naturally occur.

Poised in meditative tranquility, the devotee experiences God's omnipresent reality.
— *Lahiri Mahasaya (guru of Sri Yukteswar)*

CHAPTER FOUR

Some Truths (Facts of Life) to Know

We can more easily be successful in our learning and growing endeavors when we have an understanding of what God is, of God's relationship to us and the world, and how we can awaken and actualize our full potential as spiritual beings. For this, here are some fundamental truths to contemplate and know.

• The essence and reality of all beings and of all aspects of nature is pure consciousness. It has no origin. It is unmodified, absolute, existence-being.

• The initial manifesting aspect of pure consciousness is God—endowed with attributes with which to emanate universes and express as souls.

• From the field of God, a self-referring energy-force (the Word, Om) flows to manifest as space, time, and consciousness-energy particles which are not-yet-matter but have the potential to manifest at fine, subtle, and gross levels to produce causal (electromagnetic), astral (vital), and physical realms. This is the primordial field of nature, the *substance* of which all things are formed, which is pervaded by Universal Mind, the basis of cosmic individuality.

•   The life (Spirit) of God interacting with the field of primordial nature individualizes as souls endowed with the characteristics and attributes of God. Souls, being individualized units or rays of God's consciousness, are not independent of God. At the core, souls are pure consciousness.

•   Three innate aspects of God's consciousness regulate cosmic forces in the field of nature. The *inclination toward expansion* produces universes. *Inertia* contains cosmic forces. *Interactions* result which produce magnetic fields and diverse forms which participate in evolutionary processes. Because unaware souls tend to perceive only some aspects of the whole of God's energy-as-nature, the universe, to them, appears to be illusory.

•   Souls identify with, and express in, the realms of nature through minds and bodies. Individual mental fields are portions of Universal Mind. Mind-identified souls interact with Universal Mind in accord with their mental states and thoughts. Universal Mind, responsive to our mental states and habits of thinking, produces corresponding or equivalent personal conditions and environmental circumstances which we perceive and experience.

•   Consciousness is inclined to expand and freely express through responsive life forms. A highly evolved brain, refined nervous system, orderly mind, and healthy body, best serves the inclination of consciousness to express its qualities and capacities. Therefore, the nurturing of total wellness, along with acquired proficiency in awakening to and maintaining superconscious states, is the best preparation for experiencing spiritual growth.

• The causes of forgetfulness of our real, spiritual nature are delusions (intellectual errors) because of unconscious identification with mind and matter. This results in blind attachments to mental-emotional states, illusions (errors of perception), habitual behaviors, relationships, and circumstances. Delusions are definitely eliminated by right understanding, spiritual awakening and growth, and flawless actualization of innate soul qualities and capacities.

• Sustained desire to spiritually awaken, know and experience the reality of God, and have awareness restored to wholeness, is powerfully influential in neutralizing attachments and weakening imaginary ego-boundaries which confine soul awareness to self-conscious states. The aspiration of the heart's (the soul's) sincere desire to know God is nurtured and supported by honest self-analysis; study to understand how to live effectively and improve functional skills in the mundane realm; unfoldment of higher knowledge (of metaphysics, that which is beyond the physical); dedicated, effective spiritual practice; and surrender in God. To be surrendered in God is to be willing to learn how to live in harmony with creative principles which ensure constructive outcomes—and to do it.

• Progressive spiritual growth proceeds from

where we are in understanding and ability to function to full illumination of consciousness. Our consciousness is illumined when no trace of delusion remains. If starting at an egocentric or self-conscious level of awareness, progress will proceed from unconscious states to semiconscious states, then to clear-minded self-conscious states, superconscious states, cosmic conscious states, states of God-consciousness, and transcendental perceptions, insights, and realizations. Awakening may be slow, more obviously progressive, or rapid. There is always the possibility of instantaneous enlightenment, in a sudden flash of insight and discovery. Hence, the recommendation to be ever alert and watchful, while confidently and patiently attending to necessary routines and duties with awareness always open to the Infinite.

• It is possible for every person, by right personal endeavor and God's grace, to experience a knowing relationship with the Infinite and live fulfilled in harmony with the rhythms and flows of nature. Grace is the activity of God's expressive life (Spirit) insistently influential to our spiritual growth, necessary psychological transformations, and harmonious adjustments of relationships and circumstances for the highest good of us and everyone.

• With spiritual awakening, the soul's innate knowledge unfolds along with abilities which allow knowledge to be constructively expressed or demonstrated. Knowledge wisely applied provides freedom from limitations of all kinds, enabling and empowering us to experience complete fulfillment of the primary purposes of life and to be agents of blessings for others.

• We are in this world to learn, to grow, and to serve the purposeful trend of evolution—to knowledgeably and enjoyably participate in the processes of life and contribute to the well-being, spiritual education, awakening, and liberation of souls.

• The capacity to completely comprehend the reality of God and life processes is innate to us, to be acknowledged, unfolded, and freely expressed.

• Rapid, progressive spiritual growth is assured by our steadfast devotion to God and commitment to the enlightenment process.

My delusion is banished and by God's grace I see the truth. I am firmly established in understanding now, with my doubts removed. I shall act according to these words of wisdom.   – *Bhagavad Gita 18:73*

CHAPTER FIVE

Kriya Yoga Meditation Techniques, Initiation into Practice, and the Way of Discipleship

Although this path of constructive, purposeful living requires total commitment to soul-centered living, regular meditation practice is emphasized because of its transformative effects upon the mind and body and the opportunities it provides the meditator to experience superconsciousness. Kriya Yoga is sometimes spoken of as "the way of Self (soul)-illumination" because its practice accelerates spiritual growth by facilitating the unfoldment of innate soul qualities and powers or abilities.

Once one is educated in basic philosophical principles and instructed (and established) in how-to-live procedures, meditation practice can be taught. Instruction for doing this includes how to prepare for meditation, and how to sit, internalize attention, concentrate without being distracted, contemplate transcendental realities, and experience episodes of superconsciousness. From the outset, one is encouraged to aspire to the highest realizations possible, and not to consider preliminary perceptions or states of awareness as the ultimate experience.

Simple mantra (Sanskrit, *manas*, "mind" or

"thinking faculty," and *tra* ("to protect" or "to take beyond") meditation is usually the first procedure taught because it is easy to learn and requires only regular, alert practice for proficiency to be acquired and benefits to be experienced. Mental listening to a mantra fascinates the meditator's attention, keeping it removed from environmental, physical, emotional, and mental sources of distraction. By focusing on the mantra, physical relaxation occurs and mental processes become orderly and quiet of their own accord.

During the practice of meditation there should be no endeavor to suppress or analyze mental processes, impress the subconscious with thoughts, create a mood or emotional state, or use imagination to produce mental illusions or hallucinations. The procedure is to withdraw attention from physical and mental-emotional states while being receptive to the possibility of experiencing spontaneous adjustments of levels of awareness so that states of clear awareness can be vividly experienced. Initial states of clear awareness are sometimes blended with mental and emotional states. As meditative proficiency improves, superconsciousness devoid of mental or emotional influences is more easily experienced. It is during interludes of tranquil superconsciousness that meditative calm can beneficially influence the mind, nervous system and body. By this, the body is energized, the nervous system is enlivened and refined, and mental faculties are refreshed. Fifteen to thirty minutes once or twice a day of this easy meditation practice is recommended for all who desire only the therapeutic results of practice. For committed spiritual aspirants, this procedure is recommended as preliminary preparation for more intensive practices.

For general purposes, any pleasant mental sound can be used as one's mantra. Suitable for this purpose is the word "God" listened to by itself, or "Om" listened to with inhalation and "God" listened to when exhaling. The procedure is most effectively learned from a competent meditation teacher and only requires a few minutes to do so. Single or multi-syllable Sanskrit mantras may also be learned. These can have the added benefit of the unique sound frequency of the specific mantra. If learned during an initiation ceremony, the special quality of energy and consciousness present during initiation can be infused into the mantra and repeatedly introduced into one's mental field and physiology when used during occasions of private meditation practice.

One of the keys to successful mantra meditation practice is to remain alert and watchful, avoiding any tendency to sleep or to drift into a state of subconscious reverie. Also to be avoided are unconsciousness, daydreaming, fantasy, and involvements with memories of past events or concerns about present circumstances. If meditating for rest and mental refreshment, the session can be concluded whenever one feels inclined to return attention to everyday routines or interests. If meditating for more profound perceptions and realizations, after an interlude at the level of conscious, tranquil poise, one can proceed with more intentional practices and contemplation procedures.

After the devotee of the Kriya Yoga path has become somewhat proficient in the practice of preliminary meditation procedures and sincere interest in psychological transformation and spiritual growth is apparent, more advanced meditation routines can be learned and practiced.

Some procedures can be learned by the meditator because of what is observed and experienced during practice. It is common for one to notice the relationship between slow, refined breathing that occurs during physical relaxation and calm mental states. One may also experience subtle energy flows in the spinal pathway or in the upper parts of the body. That awareness becomes naturally established in the higher brain and at the center between and above the eyebrows, may be experienced. Awareness that one is other than mental-emotional or physical processes may be pronounced. Perception of light may occur—as a mass of clear, white light in the brain or as varied light perceptions at the spiritual eye center in the forehead. Preliminary perceptions of this kind may be due to electrical activity in the brain, elicited because of internalized focusing of attention and the influence of upward flowing vital forces. These can be allowed to attract the meditator's attention as a focusing practice, but should not be thought of as supernatural phenomena.

Subtle sounds may also be discerned in the interior of the ears or in the head. At first, these may be merely echoes of environmental sounds resonating in the ear chambers. One may also discern subtle, physical electric sounds, or finer sound perceptions of vital force frequencies. These, if heard, can be used as one uses a mantra: listened to, and eventually discarded when awareness becomes clear and soul-centeredness is established. When contemplating inner sounds, it can be helpful to remember that all sound frequencies are variations of the primordial sound-current pervading the field of nature: the Word or Om. Mindful of this, the meditator endeavors to go beyond preliminary sound perceptions to clear sounds, and beyond them to soundlessness. There are other meditation techniques which can be learned and practiced which enable one to more specifically work with inner light and sound.

The basic, advanced meditation technique taught and practiced in the Kriya Yoga tradition is a process which enables the meditator to direct flows of life force through the vital centers in the spinal pathway. This is attended by a specific breathing practice. The entire process balances the body's life forces, cleanses the blood of carbon, enlivens the nervous system, and awakens dormant soul forces. This technique is sometimes referred to as Kriya Yoga. While it is a *kriya* (action), it is only one of many practices which comprise this way to facilitate authentic spiritual growth—all of which are important to know and apply. To designate this technique as a meditation practice, I refer to it as Kriya Yoga Pranayama.

Prana (Sanskrit, "first unit of life force") is the vital power enlivening nature. Soul force enlivening the physical body is also prana. The portion of soul force in the body that is not yet awakened represents our "dormant potential" or *kundalini*. Wholesome living, the cultivation of psychological health, creativity, improvement of intellectual powers, devotion to noble ideals and to God, and aspiration to spiritual growth, contribute to the awakening of our dormant potential. Devotional prayer, the practice of superconscious meditation, and use of specific meditation techniques can directly effect an awakening of this force. As its actions become influential, regenerative energies are awakened in the body, mental powers are strengthened, the intellect becomes more discerning, and insightful, spontaneous unfoldments of soul awareness occur with increasing frequency.

Vital forces may also be aroused within us as a result of our being in harmonious relationship with others who are already spiritually awake. Their dynamic vital forces interact with ours to facilitate this experience. Initial awakening is only the beginning of the transformation process; we then have to continue to live with conscious intention to nurture spiritual growth.

Constructive psychological and physiological changes are caused by the actions of our awakened vital forces. Because of this, it is important that devotees in whom these regenerative forces are active adhere to balanced lifestyle routines, cultivate soul contentment and even-mindedness, obtain adequate rest, and provide the body with a nutrient-rich diet.

The novice practitioner of Kriya Pranayama is usually advised to practice the technique twelve times once or twice a day. Only a few minutes are required to complete the practice before settling into an extended duration of meditative contemplation. For prolonged meditation sessions of thirty minutes to an hour or more, alternative techniques can also be used whenever such practice will be helpful to maintaining a state of alert inwardness.

As the devotee progresses in proficiency and experience, other meditation techniques may be learned and practiced for the purpose of improving concentration, for contemplation of subtle states of consciousness, and for experiencing refined superconscious states and pure consciousness.

All intentional meditative procedures and techniques are but preparation for spontaneous, sustained contemplation which occurs when attention is withdrawn from involvements with sensory and mental processes. Since the soul's innate urge is to have awareness restored to wholeness, when conditions which formerly restricted this process are no longer influential, awakening to Self-knowledge naturally happens.

Preliminary superconscious states mixed with mental-emotional influences are followed by adjustments of levels of awareness which allow more refined superconsciousness, which, in turn, are replaced by pure superconscious states. When a degree of superconscious awareness can be maintained during ordinary waking hours, episodes of cosmic awareness are experienced. These occasions of intuitive perception allow one to apprehend all aspects and actions of the universe as occurring within the wholeness-field of consciousness.

Intuitive insights can, at any time, provide

direct knowledge of ourselves as spiritual beings and of our relationship with God and the universe. Flawless knowledge of God and of cosmic processes can unfold because it innately exists within us. We can utilize acquired information about spiritual growth processes to serve our personal needs until innate knowledge blossoms and is actualized. We learn first from others, then progress on the awakening path to levels of awareness and understanding which allow our spiritual capacities to be expressive.

While new on the spiritual learning and awakening path, it can be helpful to have the advice and encouragement of a teacher or *guru* (literally, "the light which removes darkness"). Such a one should be qualified as a result of having acquired proficiency because of practice, and illumination of consciousness because of being Self-realized. In matters which relate to our circumstantial, psychological, and spiritual well-being, it is useful to avoid involvements with anyone or any system of philosophy or practice which is less than the very best that is available to us.

If it is not possible to have such an ideal relationship, one can proceed with a program of self-learning: reading inspired literature and applying what is learned for the purpose of proving the principles of the teachings by personal experience. With or without a formal teacher-student or guru-disciple relationship, the inner relationship is always that of soul-to-God interaction. The outer teacher or guru is the wise counselor and spiritual friend; that which removes darkness from the mind and liberates the soul is the light of consciousness. A discerning devotee of God will avoid "spiritual teachers" who are not themselves aware of the fact that they are but agents of a Higher Power.

Instruction in spiritual practices may also be given to one during a formal initiation service or ceremony. To be *initiated* is to experience a "new beginning." During initiation into Kriya Yoga practices* the devotee is instructed in philosophy, constructive lifestyle routines, and meditation practices. Depending upon the devotee's preparedness, mantra, Kriya Yoga Pranayama, sound and light contemplation, and supplemental techniques are taught. The initiate may experience a quickening of inner forces at this time. Thereafter, the devotee is to be attentive to recommended practices, live with enlightened (knowledgeable) purpose, and in all ways remain committed to the path of light.

In the Kriya Yoga tradition, the person who initiates others into these procedures is a practicing Kriya disciple authorized by his or her guru to do so. In this way, the teachings are accurately conveyed and the spiritual force of God through the lineage of gurus is purely transmitted to the new initiate. If a person without direct attunement with the lineage of gurus presumes to initiate others into these practices, information only, even though valid,

---

* Formal initiation into these spiritual practices, along with instruction in the basic meditation techniques, is offered at our summer retreat programs and in cities and communities in the U.S. and other countries I visit. Preparatory studies are available.

is communicated without the potency of the spiritual force which should otherwise be present and available.

It is not for the purpose of controlling others or for reasons of secrecy that the tradition of transmission through an unbroken line of initiates is maintained; it is to ensure that the teachings and practices remain unadulterated and effective. There is an abundance of general philosophical and self-help information readily available. What is not so readily accessible is accurate information intentionally communicated with transformative, empowering spiritual influence.

I experienced dramatic inner awakening a few weeks after meeting my guru, Paramahansa Yogananda, and was initiated into Kriya Yoga meditation practices shortly thereafter. In late 1951, a few months before his transition from the body, he ordained me to teach in this tradition and to initiate others—which I have faithfully continued to do as my spiritual duty.

The benefits of right living and attentive spiritual practice are available to all people who choose to avail themselves of them. For individuals who sincerely feel this path to be their destined one, commitment to discipleship is recommended. The words *disciple* and *discipline* are traced to Latin *discipulus*, from *discere*, to learn. Without both a capacity and a willingness to learn, discipleship is impossible.

Characteristics which preclude success on the discipleship path are: 1) arrogance grounded in egoism; 2) disrespect for the teaching or the teacher;

3) mental perversity—the persistent habit of distorting information for self-serving purposes; 4) a pronounced neurotic or psychotic condition; 5) inability to comprehend philosophical concepts; 6) laziness; 7) addictive behaviors one is unwilling to renounce; and any other condition or circumstance that is, or is allowed to be, an obstacle to learning and successful endeavor. The purpose of discipleship is to be focused on matters essential to the fulfillment of all of life's primary purposes, including awakening to Self-knowledge and God-realization.

Once resolved on the discipleship path, our appropriate behaviors, constructive actions, and progressive spiritual growth experiences confirm our understanding and commitment. We perform all duties cheerfully and skillfully, adhere to lifestyle routines which are entirely wholesome and supportive, render caring service to others and the planet, maintain a regular schedule of devoted spiritual practice, and are content to live soul-centered and God-surrendered. In harmony with the creative principles of life that determine ideal unfoldments and the supportive inclinations and forces of nature, we are supremely happy.

When we conclude our present sojourn in space and time, only one thing will matter: how wisely and well we have lived while here. A life well lived is alone worthy of us, and is its own reward. An unfulfilled life is devoid of meaning; a God-provided opportunity wasted and a grievous disappointment to the soul. If we are not yet living with higher understanding, at our innermost level of being we yearn to do so. When this yearning to awaken to discovery of the truth about ourselves in relationship with God and to the world is allowed by us to be influential, adjustments of mental states and states of consciousness occur which remove our awareness from the darkness of unknowing. Fields of knowledge formerly inaccessible are then open to us and we can consciously choose—and live—the path of light which removes every obstacle from our lives and reveals all things necessary for us to know, and more.

It is my wish for every reader of this book that the hope that springs eternal in every soul, for clearing and expansion of awareness and unveiling of understanding that makes possible permanent freedom, will be lovingly nurtured and gloriously fulfilled by your dedicated, personal endeavors and God's abundant blessing-grace.

Kriya Yoga, this direct way of God-realization, will ultimately spread to all lands, and aid in harmonizing the nations because of humanity's personal, transcendental perceptions of the Infinite.

– Mahavatar Babaji

An Invitation to Spiritual Growth

The purpose of this brief book is to provide the reader with a basic understanding of the philosophy, teachings, and practices of this timeless way to self-discovery and authentic spiritual growth. By adopting the recommended practices and lifestyle routines here explained, anyone can definitely derive immense personal benefit. Readers who wish to engage in further study and more intentional practice are invited to request a free literature packet, with information about available publications and retreat and seminar schedules offered at our northeast Georgia retreat center, in various cities of North America, and some other countries.

If you are interested in more comprehensive study and practice of Kriya Yoga, Mr. Davis' major book on the theme, *Life Surrendered in God*—with his commentary on Patanjali's *Yoga Sutras*, is recommended. It is available from our publishing department. Also available are printed lessons for learning and practicing routines and meditation procedures as preparation for initiation.

Center for Spiritual Awareness
Post Office Box 7
Lakemont, Georgia 30552 (U.S.A.)

(706) 782-4723 weekdays   Fax (706) 782-4560 anytime

Our international headquarters and retreat center
is located on Lake Rabun Road in Lakemont, Georgia.

A Sharing Opportunity

Please share copies of this
introduction to the philosophy and practices
of Kriya Yoga with others whom you know to
be sincerely interested in spiritual growth.

2–10 copies, $1.50 each
11–49 copies, $1.30 each
50 or more, $1.00 each.

Postage free in the U.S.
Postage outside the U.S., include $2.00
plus 20 cents per book.

Use our address or telephone numbers as
they appear on the preceding page.

Booksellers may order at usual trade discounts.